EXPLORING CAREERS

Police Officer

Peggy J. Parks

KIDHAVEN PRESS™

THOMSON

GALE

San Diego • Detroit • New York • San Francisco • Cleveland
New Haven, Conn. • Waterville, Maine • London • Munich

© 2003 by KidHaven Press. KidHaven Press is an imprint of The Gale Group, Inc.,
a division of Thomson Learning, Inc.

KidHaven™ and Thomson Learning™ are trademarks used herein under license.

For more information, contact
KidHaven Press
27500 Drake Rd.
Farmington Hills, MI 48331-3535
Or you can visit our Internet site at http://www.gale.com

LIBRARY OF CONGRESS CATALOGING-IN-PUBLICATION DATA

Parks, Peggy J., 1951–
    Police officer / by Peggy J. Parks.
    p. cm.—(Exploring careers series)
    Includes bibliographical references.
    Contents: Different kinds of police officers—What it takes to be a police
officer—In the station and on the street—Meet a police sergeant.
    ISBN 0-7377-1486-7 (lib.: alk. paper)
    1.Police—United States—Juvenile literature. [1. Police. 2. Occupations.]
I. Title. II. Series.
HV7922.P37 2003
363.2—dc21

2002009139

Printed in the United States of America

CONTENTS

CHAPTER 1

Different Kinds of Police Officers

Police officers have an important job to do, and that is to keep people safe. It is not an easy job because even though there are laws designed to protect society, there are also people who break them. When they do, it is up to police officers to catch them and stop them from committing more crimes. Also, there are times when accidents happen that may involve no crime, but still require police officers to help.

Uniformed Officers

Police officers who work for city police departments are called patrol officers or police officers, and often they are called cops. They wear uniforms so people can immediately identify them as police, and they carry guns so they can protect themselves and other people in dangerous situations.

The number of patrol officers who work for city police departments depends on the size of the city or town. For instance, Chicago, the third largest city in the United States, employs over thirteen thousand officers. The small town of Independence, Louisiana, has only about six.

Patrol officers get around in many different ways. Most travel the traditional way, in marked police cars, while some ride in unmarked cars. There are officers who ride motorcycles and others, known as beat cops, who patrol neighborhoods on foot. Plus, many large cities have officers who patrol from the

Patrol officers, like these uniformed cops, patrol neighborhoods both on foot and in marked vehicles.

air in police helicopters. Los Angeles, California, has the largest flying police squad in the world: fifteen helicopters and ninety officers who fly in them twenty-four hours a day, every day of the week.

Some patrol officers cover their areas on bicycles. One advantage of bike travel is that officers can approach crime suspects without being seen or heard, so they are often able to catch the suspects before they can run away. Also, bicycles can go places where cars cannot go, such as through parks and into narrow alleys. A bicycle unit at the Orange, California, police department is composed of six officers, who spend ten hours a day riding throughout the city on specially equipped mountain bikes. There are also police departments with mounted units, or teams of patrol officers who travel around on horses. Officers on horseback are approximately nine feet above the ground, so they are able to see greater distances and are more visible to others than officers on foot or in cars. In New York City, mounted officers patrol many different areas including Central Park, Coney Island's boardwalk, Times Square, and Yankee Stadium.

The Role of a Sheriff

Like patrol officers, sheriffs wear uniforms and respond to calls for help. Their duties are almost identical to city patrol officers. However, the areas they cover are spread throughout counties rather than in cities. Because their areas are often quite

Radar unit

Laptop computer

Mobile vision camera

Video monitor

Field radio

TALON

Photo courtesy of Sgt. Richard Russo/Hoffman Estates Police Department.

Radar remote control

Lights, siren controls

Local police band radio

large, sheriffs generally travel in cars. Some sheriff departments also have bike units, mounted units, and helicopter units.

The officers who work for sheriff departments are often called deputies. One person, usually elected by the people who live in the county, serves as the sheriff. Most sheriff departments are smaller than city police departments, but their size depends on the size of the county. Florida's Palm Beach County covers nearly twenty-four hundred square miles, and the sheriff department is large, with over one thousand officers.

Bicycles allow police officers to patrol areas where large vehicles cannot go.

The State Police

Officers who work for state police departments are usually called state troopers or highway patrol officers. They wear uniforms and carry badges that identify them as working for the state police, and like other police officers, they also carry guns. State troopers are responsible for watching over the nation's highways by enforcing speed limit laws and answering calls for help. They also provide assistance to local police and sheriff departments.

Many state police departments have specialized divisions. For instance, a scuba diving team responds to suspected drownings and life-threatening incidents in the water. Explosive teams respond to bomb threats, and they are often accompanied by dogs that are trained to sniff out explosives. Emergency response teams deal with high-risk incidents such as

Some police officers work with specially trained bomb-sniffing dogs like this basset hound.

Bomb squad police remove a suspicious suitcase from a hotel. Their work is often dangerous.

prison disturbances or **hostage** situations. Helicopter teams handle aerial searches for **fugitives** and victims, and assess disasters. **Narcotics** teams specialize in investigating illegal drug activities.

One example of a state police specialized unit is the Texas Department of Public Safety's Narcotics

Service division. The group employs three hundred officers who are trained to investigate drug-related crimes. These crimes include drugs that are smuggled across the Texas/Mexico border via the state's highways, underwater, or through the air.

Detectives

Police officers who handle assignments that need in-depth investigation are called detectives. These officers wear regular clothes instead of uniforms. They have been promoted to detective positions after serving as officers for a period of time, usually a few years. Detectives may work for city police departments, state police departments, or sheriff departments. Even though they do not wear uniforms, they carry badges that identify them as police officers. They also carry guns, which they keep in shoulder or belt holsters.

Unlike uniformed officers, who are the first to report to the scene of a crime, detectives are brought in when additional facts are needed to solve a case. They find these facts by collecting **evidence** that helps them determine if the person (or persons) suspected of committing a crime is guilty.

Detectives often specialize in one or more types of crime. For instance, a big-city police department might have some detectives who specialize in burglary or **homicide**. Or detectives might handle narcotics cases, while others specialize in crimes like rape or prostitution. Some detectives work only on

A team of detectives frisks two suspects for weapons before arresting them.

crimes that involve juveniles, or young people under the age of eighteen.

Government Cops

Just as city, county, and state police detectives investigate crime in their assigned areas, officers who work for the **FBI** are detectives who investigate crime for the federal government. Sometimes called "the Feds," FBI agents investigate serious crimes such as kidnapping, drug trafficking from one state to another, attacks of terrorism, or **air piracy**.

Another high-profile crime that FBI agents investigate is **espionage**, which involves **spy** activities. When FBI agents investigate spies, they must watch for things like phony names and jobs that are used to hide a person's secret activities. They must also be on the lookout for sophisticated gadgets used by spies, such as tiny cameras that are easily concealed.

No matter what branch of law enforcement they work in, the men and women who serve as police officers are necessary to help protect people's lives and property. Because of the work they do, the nation's cities, highways, streets, and neighborhoods are much safer places.

CHAPTER 2

What It Takes to Be a Police Officer

Police officers' jobs require that they have personal qualities such as honesty and integrity, and a genuine willingness to help people. They must also be skilled and trained to handle many different kinds of emergencies. They learn about these things during their training, usually at police academies, and some also attend college to study criminal justice. However, police officers learn most of what they need to know by actually doing their jobs.

Keeping Their Cool

When they are on the job, police officers often face the unknown. Even when there are no obvious signs of danger, officers know that trouble can erupt quickly. When that happens, police officers must remain calm and in control, even when they feel angry or afraid.

Domestic assault can create dangerous situations for police officers. When officers are called to a home where violence has been reported, they are likely to face angry people. Sometimes those people have weapons. Former police officer Bob Johnson says that cops must remain cool and calm in these situations. They must keep their composure, and no matter how angry people are, officers must avoid getting angry themselves, as he explains: "You speak in a calm voice and use slow, deliberate hand gestures, avoiding any sudden movements that could

Police cadets practice storming a warehouse during their training.

Police officers restrain two angry boys after responding to a domestic violence call.

be interpreted as aggressive or hostile. In a domestic assault case, it's up to the police officer to help people get their anger under control, not to take sides, and to avoid using force if at all possible."[1] Johnson adds that the police officer's goal is to diffuse people's anger, and to keep the situation from becoming any worse than it already is.

Handling Medical Emergencies

Almost all police officers, whether they work for a city, state, or county, are trained to handle medical emergencies. This is important because when there has been an accident or crime involving injuries, police officers may arrive at the scene before emergency medical personnel. In these situations, they must be able to evaluate a patient's condition, stop any bleeding, and if necessary, perform **CPR** and other lifesaving measures.

Michael Lorenz is a Michigan state trooper who saved the life of a man who had stopped breathing. Lorenz and another trooper were at the police station when the emergency call came in. They grabbed their first aid kit, jumped in their patrol car, and got to the man's house as quickly as they could. He explains what happened next:

A sheriff's deputy assists firefighters in administering CPR to an injured soccer player.

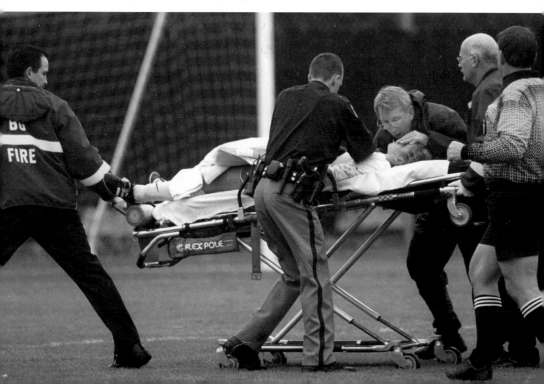

"When we got there, the man wasn't breathing and we found that he had no pulse. We immediately started CPR, and kept it up until the paramedics arrived about five minutes later. By that time, he had regained his ability to breathe, and he was taken to the hospital. Two or three weeks later, he came by the police post to thank us for saving his life."[2]

High-Speed Chases

Television cop shows often feature high-speed chases. Police cars and fleeing vehicles race through crowded city streets as they run red lights and recklessly dodge traffic. In real life, however, these chases do not happen that often because police know they are very dangerous. In fact, almost 40 percent of high-speed chases end in crashes and many result in injuries, sometimes even in death.

If police officers have to chase a fleeing suspect, they must use extreme caution and good judgment. For instance, officers are more likely to engage in a chase on a highway, where there are open stretches of road. There are more cars and more people in the middle of cities, so the likelihood of a crash and injuries is greater.

One way that police officers can minimize the length of a chase is to force fleeing cars to stop with **spike strips**. Officers use their radios to call ahead and alert other officers that a suspect is approaching. The officers who receive the call place spike strips on

A firefighter and police officer struggle to remove the driver from the wreckage of a car that crashed during a high-speed chase.

the road. When the car runs over the strips, the tires pop and the car is forced to stop. This happened in April 2002 when a fifteen-year-old Nevada boy made threats to blow up his school, and then hijacked a school bus. In trying to get away from the police, the boy broke through a roadblock, rammed into a patrol car, and then led police on a high-speed chase across the desert. Spike strips on the highway in front of him brought the bus to a stop, and the boy was arrested.

When to Use Firearms

Whether to engage in high-speed chases is one area where police officers need to use good judgment. Another is whether or not they should draw their weapons. Actually, gun use by police officers

The stun gun (pictured) delivers a powerful electrical shock that can temporarily paralyze a suspect.

is less common than people think. Many officers go through their entire careers without pulling a gun on another person.

Sometimes officers use weapons that are not deadly, but are powerful enough to subdue a suspect. One such weapon is pepper spray, which causes severe burning and stinging in the eyes, and can also cause temporary blindness. Other non-deadly weapons are **stun guns** and **taser guns**. These weapons shoot an electrical charge instead of bullets, so they can temporarily paralyze a suspect's muscles. (Stun guns and taser guns are illegal in some states.)

If an officer does find it necessary to fire a gun, police departments conduct investigations to make sure the officer acted properly. In 1999, two San Diego police officers shot and killed a man after he had become violent with them. They tried using pepper spray, but it had no effect on him. They tried to wrestle him to the ground and get handcuffs on him, but he continued to fight back. Witnesses later said that the man was very large and muscular, and was also under the influence of

Police officers must use good judgment when pulling a gun on someone.

alcohol and drugs. After the officers shot the man, the San Diego district attorney investigated the case. He determined that the officers' lives were in danger, so it was necessary for them to use their guns to defend themselves.

In addition to knowing when to fire their guns, police officers must also be able to disarm potential shooters. A detective in Carson City, Nevada, was chasing a fugitive when the man abruptly turned and stopped in front of her. She ran into him, and he grabbed the pistol from her holster and pointed it at her. Suddenly she was staring into the barrel of her own gun, and she feared for her life. However, she managed to wrestle the gun away from him.

These are just a few of the situations that police officers face when they are working. To do their jobs well, they must have the right combination of personal qualities, professional training, and real-world experience. The longer they work at their jobs, the more experienced they become—and the more valuable they are to society.

CHAPTER 3

In the Station and on the Street

Police officers' specific tasks differ based on whether they are patrol officers, sheriffs, state troopers, detectives, or FBI agents. They all have one thing in common, however. When they go to work, they never know quite what to expect because anything can happen.

Guarding Cities and Counties

Police officers and sheriffs spend much of their time on patrol, responding to calls for help. A typical day for these officers usually starts with briefing meetings, where they learn about the latest crime activity, department updates, and other information. Then they go out and patrol their assigned areas. When they are called to the scene of a crime or an accident, they interview witnesses and victims, gather evidence, and record their findings. Later, back at the station, they will write reports about what happened during their shift.

Rick Mulcahy is a police officer in Fayetteville, North Carolina. He does not drive a car; rather, he patrols his section of the city on horseback. One of Mulcahy's duties is to watch for drivers who exceed the speed limit. When they drive by, he gauges their speed by pointing a handheld radar gun at their vehicle. He says most people are sur-

Police officers, such as these special operations officers, often start their day with a brief meeting.

How a Police Radar Gun Works

① Radar gun broadcasts radio waves at a moving vehicle.

② Radio waves strike vehicle and are reflected back to the radar gun.

③ A computer in the radar gun calculates the speed of the car.

Radio waves sent
Radio waves reflected

prised that police officers can monitor speed when they are riding horses. One stop he made involved a pickup truck that was traveling fifty-seven miles per hour in a forty-five-mile-per-hour zone. He stopped the truck by riding his horse into the middle of the road and holding up his hand. The driver pulled over, and Mulcahy and his horse trotted over to take the man's driver's license and registration. He then tied his horse behind the truck while he wrote the ticket.

At the State Level

State troopers are responsible for enforcing highway traffic laws, which includes issuing tickets to drivers who violate the law by speeding. They also provide assistance at the scene of highway accidents by directing traffic and giving first aid to people who are injured.

However, state troopers do much more than just patrol highways. They are frequently called on to assist other police and sheriff departments who may need help with accidents or crimes. Plus, in small towns or rural areas that do not have their own police departments, state troopers often handle all law enforcement duties.

Trooper Lorenz is based in Alpena, a small lakeshore town located in Michigan. He says that all troopers spend some time patrolling the highways, but the majority of their time is spent re-

State troopers issue a speeding ticket to the driver of this sports car.

sponding to calls for help. These officers investigate all kinds of crimes, from knocked-down mailboxes to murders, from breaking and entering (B&E) cases to domestic assault, and everything in between. One particular B&E case that Lorenz handled involved some teenagers who were breaking into cars. He explains what happened when he and his partner caught them: "We found that they had broken into maybe forty different cars that night. We looked through the property they had stolen—things like cell phones, stereos, and CDs—and we found a laptop computer, which we tracked to a different city in Michigan. We contacted the sheriff department there, and found that the kids had broken into hundreds of other cars and hadn't been caught."[3] By solving this case, Lorenz and other police officers were able to solve prior cases, too. He says that is the way it often works in law enforcement.

Investigating Crime

When a crime has occurred, police officers go to the scene to find out what happened. If they cannot solve the crime at the scene, or if the criminals got away, the case is assigned to a detective for further investigation.

Sergeant Louis Fata has been a detective in Miami Beach, Florida, for over ten years. He has investigated crimes such as missing persons, murders, robberies, and gang-related incidents. His investigations typically

Police officers gather evidence after raiding the home of a suspected drug dealer.

involve working with crime-scene technicians, supervising what should and should not be picked up and what photographs need to be taken. He describes a typical crime scene after a bank robbery: "I may go to the scene to see where the criminals entered the bank. I look to see if they left a cigarette end behind. Did they drop anything coming to the crime scene or as they left? In one case, a crook threw his gun into a sewer a few blocks from the scene when he saw a police car coming. Police recovered the gun and used it as evidence."[4] Fata spends a lot of time in his office, reading reports and making phone calls, and then he interviews suspects, witnesses, and victims. Once he has gathered all the evidence he needs,

Special operations officers share information about a crime scene.

he prepares crime reports. He says that the most rewarding thing about his job is when he can solve cases and help get criminals off the streets.

High-Profile Crimes

Like detectives, FBI agents investigate cases to help solve them. However, the cases they work on involve high-profile crimes that happen anywhere in the country. One of these crimes occurred in March 2002, when a California businessman was kidnapped and held for **ransom**. The local police called the FBI, who immediately began investigating. Two weeks later they found the kidnapping victim tied up in a motel room with tape over his eyes and mouth. He was badly shaken from his experience, but he was alive and safe.

FBI agents also travel to foreign countries to investigate crimes that in some way affect the United States. One such case happened in 1998, when a bomb exploded near the U.S. embassy in Nairobi, **Kenya**. The bomb killed 212 people, including 12 Americans, and wounded as many as 5,000 others. The embassy was nearly destroyed, and since it was located in a crowded downtown area, surrounding buildings were also damaged. FBI agents went to Nairobi to assist with the investigation, and to help with search and rescue efforts. Over a period of many months, the agents conducted over one thousand investigative interviews. Their efforts contributed toward the arrest

A squad car riddled with bullet holes is pulled from a roadside ditch. A police officer's job is often dangerous.

of over a dozen suspects, and led to the convictions of four men who were sentenced to life in federal prison.

Whether they patrol a state highway or walk a city beat, work for a sheriff department or investigate

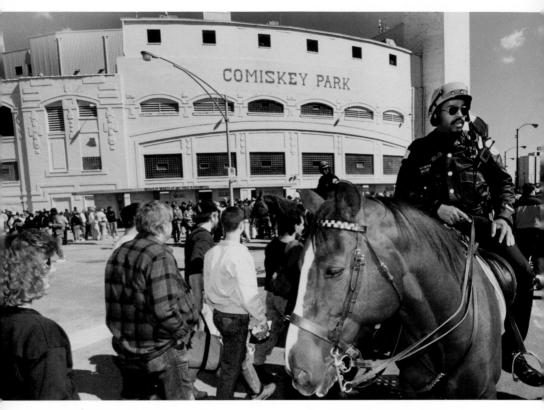

A mounted police officer monitors a crowd of sports fans outside a baseball stadium.

crimes for the U.S. government, police officers work very hard. Their jobs are often rewarding, but they can also be dangerous and stressful. Their specific tasks may differ, but all police officers have one thing in common: a commitment to protect people and enforce the law.

CHAPTER 4

Meet a Police Sergeant

Stan Kid has been a police officer for twenty-eight years, and a police sergeant since 1985. He works for the Malverne Police Department in Long Island, New York. As a sergeant, he supervises the day-to-day duties of six or seven police officers. He spends most of his time in his precinct office, and he also likes to spend a few hours each day out on the street where he patrols in an unmarked police car. Sergeant Kid shares his thoughts about police work:

> I decided to join the police force because I knew it would give me the ability to work with people, to help people, and be of some good. Also, my brother was a cop before me and I was proud of what he was doing for a living.
>
> What I like best about working in law enforcement is the respect that comes with the job. As

much as people complain about cops, in general, they still respect us and they show it. The other side is, we have to earn that respect—we have to earn it every day.[5]

Most Heartwarming Experience

Sergeant Kid says there have been many times when he has found his job rewarding. When he thinks about his most heartwarming experiences, one incident in particular comes to mind:

A few years ago I was waiting at a traffic light and a car pulled up beside me. The driver rolled down

A police sergeant (left) talks with an off-duty officer. Police sergeants supervise lower-ranking police officers.

the window and asked, "Are you Sergeant Kid?" I said yes, and he said, "I'm sure you don't remember me, but about twenty years ago you carried my son to the hospital after he was hit by a car." I remembered his son immediately. An elderly woman had lost control of her car, accidentally veered up onto the lawn where the boy had been playing, and rolled over him. He was in bad shape and I didn't know how quickly the ambulance would get there, so I scooped him up in my arms, and my partner drove us to the hospital. The man told me that he and his family had moved away and were back in New York for a visit, and he said, "We just thought you'd like to know that our son graduated from dental school this year. We also wanted to thank you again for saving his life." That warmed my heart. When you get to help a child who's been hurt, and the child grows up healthy, it's a wonderful feeling.

The Tough Times

Sergeant Kid says that just like any job, being a cop is not always fun:

Some of the worst times are when you have to deal with irate people. They're mad about something, like they had a fight with a coworker or an argument with their spouse, and you spot them driving like a lunatic. You pull them over because you have to, and they start in on you, saying things like, "What, you've got nothing else to do but hassle me?" You know they're really mad at someone other than you. You're just the convenient person for them to take out their anger on. Still, those situations are not fun.

Because Sergeant Kid is a supervisor, he is responsible for the officers who work for him. He says that most of the time he enjoys his supervision duties, but not always: "I don't like it when I have to chastise the officers who work for me. Fortunately, this doesn't happen very often. My motto is, don't get me in trouble, don't get yourselves in trouble, and don't hurt anybody unless it's absolutely necessary. For the most part, I like being in charge. It has its benefits. But it's not always easy."

Facing Danger

Sergeant Kid, like all police officers, has found himself in dangerous situations. He talks about one incident that he found especially frightening:

Before I became a sergeant, I was out on patrol duty one night and heard on my radio about a stolen car. Another police car was in pursuit, but I spotted the stolen vehicle and tried to block it by parking my car across the road as a roadblock—which was a dumb thing to do. The driver was going maybe eighty miles per hour, and as soon as I saw his lights bearing down on me, I knew he planned to crash into my car. I quickly pulled forward, but the car ran into me, spinning my car around. The collision also sent the stolen car careening down the road, and when it stopped, the driver and one passenger jumped out and ran off into the woods. Another cop chased them on foot

A police sergeant (right) briefs his officers before a sting operation.

and fired a warning shot in the air, but he never did catch them.

The Tragedy of September 11

When Sergeant Kid looks back on his twenty-eight years as a cop, he says he has witnessed many things, both good and bad. On September 11, 2001, after two jets crashed into the World Trade Center in New York City, he worked as part of the rescue team. He describes the experience.

No matter what I've gone through in my life, that day I knew, firsthand, that I had experienced hell. When I first arrived on the scene, all I could think of was that it couldn't possibly be real. It was like a Batman movie, with its eerie, gothic, dark view of Gotham City. It was dark even in the daylight because of the smoke and dust in the awful-smelling air. I spent days working with other police officers, firefighters, emergency medical crews, military personnel, and civilian volunteers as we dug through twisted steel, cement chunks, airplane parts, and occasional personal belongings. We all had the same goal—working together to seek both the living and the dead. Each of us was desperate to find someone, to help someone.

As horrible as this experience was, I also saw humanity at its finest. I saw hundreds of men and women who were doing everything humanly possible to find everyone. I saw these people working together with no recognition of difference in occupation, sex, race, or color. No one seemed to see anyone as other than a fellow human being who was dealing with an unthinkable tragedy. And each and every one of them kept going until the job was done. These people are true heroes, and I'm so very proud to have met them and to have the honor of standing side by side with them.

Parting Words

As for what message he would like to pass along to kids, Sergeant Kid has this to say: "Remember that police officers are there to help you. You've probably been taught not to talk to strangers, but cops are *not* strangers, and you can always depend on them. Some people say that cops are there to put bad people away, but that's only part of the story: Cops are there to stop bad people from doing anything bad to you."

The horrible events of September 11, 2001, tested even the finest police officers.

A police officer assists a lost girl.

He adds this about a career as a police officer: "If you think you might like to be a cop when you grow up, by all means do so. It could give you an opportunity to make a positive difference in people's lives, and to change your own life for the better, as well."

NOTES

Chapter 2: What It Takes to Be a Police Officer

1. Bob Johnson, interview with author, May 28, 2002.
2. Michael Lorenz, interview with author, May 31, 2002.

Chapter 3: In the Station and on the Street

3. Lorenz, interview with author.
4. Quoted in "Meet Detective Fata," *Kids Discover,* July 1999, p. 14.

Chapter 4: Meet a Police Sergeant

5. All quotes in Chapter 4: Stan Kid, interview with author, May 23, 2002.

GLOSSARY

air piracy: Airline hijacking.

CPR: Cardiopulmonary resuscitation, a lifesaving technique that involves chest compressions and rescue breathing.

domestic assault: Crime that involves people from the same household threatening or physically harming each other.

espionage: The practice of spying or using spies to obtain information.

evidence: Something that furnishes proof of a crime, such as fingerprints or other clues.

FBI: Federal Bureau of Investigation.

fugitive: An escaped criminal.

homicide: Murder.

hostage: A person taken by force and held against his or her will.

Kenya: A republic in eastern Africa.

narcotics: Illegal drugs, such as marijuana, cocaine, heroin, or Ecstasy.

ransom: Something that is demanded (usually money) for the release of something or someone from captivity.

spike strips: Strips with pointed spikes that can be laid across a road to stop fleeing vehicles.

spy: A person who secretly watches another person or thing to get information.

stun gun: A weapon that shoots an electrical charge, instead of bullets, when it is pressed against someone.

taser gun: A weapon that is similar to a stun gun, but does not have to be held against someone. When the trigger is pulled, it shoots a cartridge that can travel fifteen to twenty feet through the air.

FOR FURTHER EXPLORATION

Books

Jonathan Rubinstein, *On the Job with a Police Officer, Protector of the Peace.* Hauppauge, NY: Barrons, 2001. The story of Hugo and Bridgit, two friends who help the police catch a purse snatcher. Because of their help, they are invited to visit police headquarters, where they learn firsthand what police officers do.

Joan Plummer Russell, *Aero and Officer Mike: Police Partners.* Honesdale, PA: Caroline House, Boyds Mills Press, 2001. The real-life story of Officer Mike Matsik and his police dog, Aero. Looks at the many tasks they handle as a team, including finding lost children and sniffing out illegal drugs, and also gives readers a glimpse at the special relationship police officers have with their canine companions.

Periodicals

Janice Arenofsky, "Crime and Punishment: From Lab to Courtroom," *Career World,* February 1996. An informative article with information about the life of a police officer. Includes examples, statistics, and salary ranges.

Mariah Christensen, "Mounted Police, Minnesota Style," *Horsepower,* June/July 1996. An article about police officers who patrol on horseback.

Jeff Csatari, "Top Gun Cruisers," *Boys' Life,* January 1994. An interesting article about the different types of fast cars police officers drive.

Websites

Cops Online (www.copsonline.com). A website created by police officers. Includes articles, photos, interesting information about law enforcement, and a collection of funny 911 calls.

Department of Justice—For Kids and Youth (www.usdoj.gov). Site features separate sections for kids, and includes a wealth of information related to safety, current events, U.S. history, and government.

Federal Bureau of Investigation—FBI for Kids (www.fbi.gov). Site includes a wealth of information about the FBI. The kids' section is divided into two parts: one for kindergarten through fifth grade, and one for sixth through twelfth grade. Kids can read about a day in the life of an FBI agent, follow the trail of a spy, and play games on the site.

National Crime Prevention Council (www.ncpc.org). Site includes "McGruff's List of Web Links," a collection of links to law enforcement–related websites for children, teens, and parents.

The Princeton Review—Police Officer Career Profile (www.review.com). Site includes a comprehensive description of police officer careers, including past and future projections, and suggested majors for college-bound students.

INDEX

WITHDRAWN